HMS DEFIANCE

Devonport's Submarine Base

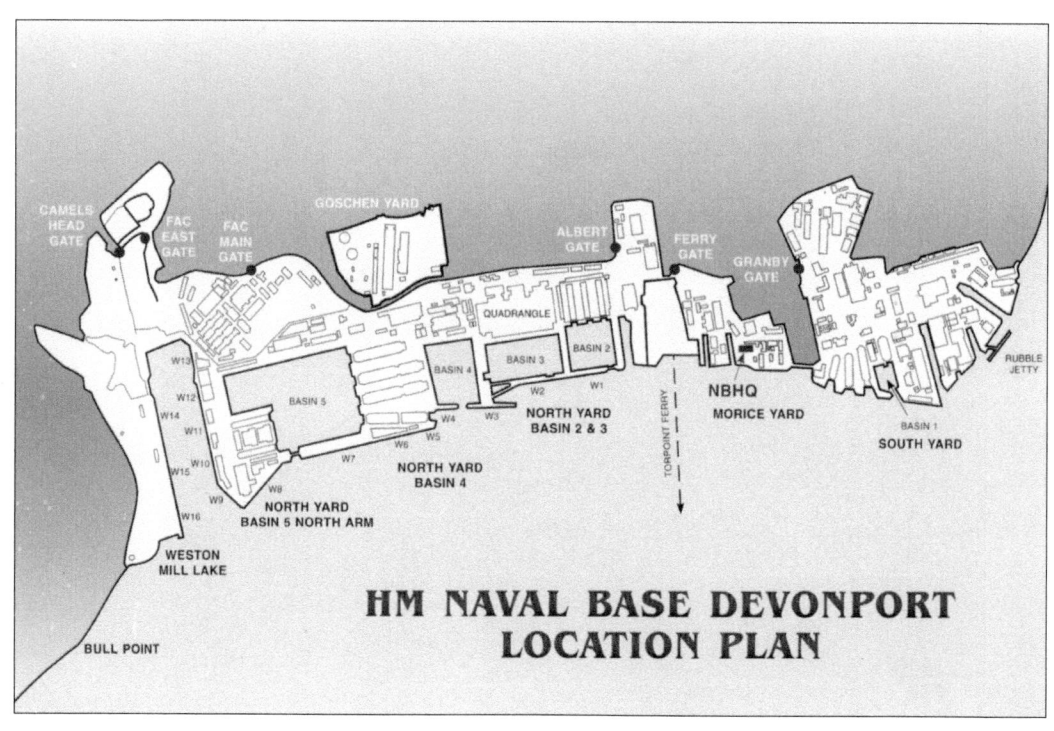

CAMELS HEAD GATE

FAC EAST GATE

FAC MAIN GATE

GOSCHEN YARD

ALBERT GATE

FERRY GATE

GRANBY GATE

RUBBLE JETTY

QUADRANGLE

BASIN 2

BASIN 3

BASIN 4

BASIN 5

W13

W12

W14

W11

W10

W15

W9

W16

W8

W7

W6

W5

W4

W3

W2

W1

NBHQ

MORICE YARD

TORPOINT FERRY

NORTH YARD BASIN 2 & 3

NORTH YARD BASIN 4

NORTH YARD BASIN 5 NORTH ARM

WESTON MILL LAKE

BULL POINT

BASIN 1

SOUTH YARD

HM NAVAL BASE DEVONPORT
LOCATION PLAN

HMS DEFIANCE

Devonport's Submarine Base

KEITH HALL

All money raised from the sale of this book is being donated to the Devonport Dockyard Museum and the Royal Naval Submarine Museum, Gosport.

First published 2008

Reprinted 2011

The History Press Ltd
The Mill, Brimscombe Port
Stroud, Gloucestershire, GL5 2QG
www.thehistorypress.co.uk

ISBN 978 0 7524 3758 3

Printed in Great Britain

CONTENTS

ACKNOWLEDGEMENTS

I would like to thank the following people for their help and assistance in compiling this book: Lt Cdr D.M. Parkinson and Mr G. Rendle from Devonport Dockyard Museum, for allowing me access to their photographic archives and keeping an 'out of area' boy straight; Mr M. Reeves; Cdr Tall and his staff at the Royal Naval Submarine Museum, Gosport, in particular Mrs Debbie Corner, the very helpful and patient 'Keeper of Photographs'; the *Navy News* for allowing to use photographs from their archives.

I am also greatly indebted to Andy Endacott for permission to rummage in and borrow from his excellent series of books (see bibliography).

My thanks also to Mr Steve Johnson and his very interesting and informative website.

I am particularly grateful to the following organisations for permission to use their photographs, and the waiving of their copyright fee:

Crown Copyright
Devonport Dockyard Ltd (now Babcock Marine)
www.cyber–heritage.co.uk
Navy News

And finally, I ask for forgiveness from any contributors who may have been unintentionally omitted from these acknowledgements.

INTRODUCTION

Plymouth has long been used as a naval base. From the town's sheltered waters such famous seaman as Drake and Raleigh sailed. Devonport Dockyard, or Plymouth Dock as it was originally known, started life in 1693 when a wet and dry dock was constructed, in what is now part of the South Yard. From these meagre beginnings, the dockyard grew into the biggest naval base in western Europe. It covers an area of some 622 acres, contains twenty-five tidal basins, five basins and twelve dry docks of varying sizes that can accommodate frigates, submarines and the through deck cruisers. In recent years a considerable investment program has ensured that the Dockyard's facilities remain up to date.

Unfortunately for the area, submarines made a belated and erratic entry on to the naval scene at Devonport, even though from the earliest seafaring days there was never any doubt that submariners would sail from Plymouth. Indeed, Sir Francis Drake himself advised sailors not to change their underwear before battle; an obvious reference to submariners.

When submarines were considered little more than harbour defence craft, the 10th Flotilla was based at Devonport on the depot ship HMS *Onyx*. During 1914 the flotilla number was changed to the 1st and during the war lost two of the flotilla submarines in the Sound.

In August 1916 the increasing number of submarines lead to a reorganisation of the flotillas. The Admiralty approved the scheme on 18 June 1916, although the actual reorganisation was not completed until 20 August of that year. All squadrons, except one, received new numbers. Flotillas 1 to 7 were employed on coastal patrol work, and were largely used for training purposes. Flotillas 8 to 13 were known as the Overseas Flotillas. The 12th and 13th Flotillas were to be formed from the K-class submarines. They were to be stationed at Scapa and Rosyth, as required by the Commander-in-Chief of the Grand Fleet. They were considered units of the Grand Fleet and, as such, were not attached to a permanent base.

When the scheme was submitted it was suggested that the 'flotilla' name be dropped to avoid confusion with the destroyer flotillas. Some of the suggestions for the new name included: Aquarilla, Squadrilla, Subtilla, Platoon, Maniple, Shoal, Array and Armada. Luckily, common sense prevailed and the name flotilla stuck, although it is said that 'Submarilla' was a firm favourite for a while.

Until the A- and T-class submarines of the 2nd Submarine Squadron and their depot ship, HMS *Forth*, arrived in Devonport in 1961, there had not been a submarine squadron based in Plymouth since the end of the First World War. However, submarines were far from a strange sight, and the dockyard built many submarines of various classes over the years.

Keith Hall
Tumbledown, Clynder

One

DEVONPORT DOCKYARD

The Royal Navy has always been considered the first line of the nation's defence. Being able to control the seas was a fundamental necessity, those which surround the islands which make up the British Isles and those further afield, the free and uninterrupted use of which the fortunes of the Empire so depended. Kings, and later politicians, quickly realised the importance of a fleet to protect the country's shores and interntional trade and also, perhaps, when the work was done, as an asset to be got rid of in an attempt to 'balance the books'. Likewise, the organisations and establishments that grew up to support this fleet, both at home and abroad, prospered and waned on a kingly or political whim.

The year AD 790 marked the first Viking attacks on the country. These presented the biggest threat to Anglo-Saxon England. The attacks ranged from small pirate-like raids to full-blown invasion and settlement. There was no navy to repel these invasions until the reign of King Alfred (871–899), who is traditionally credited with organising the first English Navy. His other naval achievements include the 'blocking' of the River Lea, thereby denying the Danes access in 895. He went on to remove the invaders from London. Despite these successes, the whole fleet ran aground during the first battle in which the fledgling English Navy fought. That aside, Alfred did unite the warring kingdoms south of the Humber, and gave life to the idea that an island can best protect itself by facing the aggressor at sea, preferably nearer to their coast than one's own. Alfred, the first English king to be dubbed 'The Great' by historians, was also the first king to make a serious attempt to 'mark the waves'; in fact the term 'Rule Britannia' dates from this period.

Around 896, Alfred ordered ships to be built to confront the Danish who were attacking the south coast of Wessex. These vessels appear to have been approximately twice as long as their Danish counterparts, with up to sixty oars. They were probably faster and more seaworthy than the Danish boats, and possibly armed with a ram in a similar manner to Mediterranean galleys. Alfred had been taken to Rome by his father, Æthelwulf, as a boy, and his design may have been influenced by ships he saw on his travels. Alfred's navy seems to have died with him. Indeed, while many medieval kings appear to have possessed a navy, they very rarely exercised a firm control over their operations. In fact, when William the Conquerer arrived at Hastings, nearly 200 years after the reign of Alfred, he landed unopposed. Harold's fleet, tired of waiting for the Norman invaders, had practically disbanded. It was also harvest time, and hands were required to gather the crops. Even if the English 'fleet' had been assembled, it would have made a less than impressive sight; their primary role appears to have been little more than acting as ferries for knights and their supporters, while the ships themselves were in reality just large open boats. The crews of these generally did not sleep on board; rather, the boats would be beached and meals cooked on board and the crews would sleep under the sails.

In the wake of 1066 the new Norman aristocracy of England were required to supply fighting men to the king's seaports, which would form the frontline if there was another invasion. Out of this understanding developed the Confederation of the Cinque Ports (the oldest maritime institution in the UK). The idea had originally been proposed by Edward the Confessor, just prior to the conquest.

Hastings, Ronney, Hythe, Dover and Sandwich were the first in the Confederation. Winikelsea, Rye and several other towns on the south-east coast were added in later years. All these ports agreed to supply the king with a number of ships and crews for a set period each year. Very few of these ships were specifically built for fighting. In return, these ports were exempt from paying tax and had other legal privileges, including freedom from such fascinating-sounding taxes as 'blodwit', 'fledwit', 'tumbrel', 'mundbryce' and 'ligan'. These ships were the main form of transport for the king's armies as they travelled to the Crusades. To ensure that the knights' superiority over seamen was maintained, wooden castles were built on the deck for'd and aft (hence the origins of the term 'forecastle').

Seafaring at this time was used both for trade – exporting wool and importing wine from the English possesion of Bordeaux – and for conveying kings and their knights to and from foreign battlefields. This remained essentially unchanged for 350 years, until Drake's circumnavigation of the world in 1580 changed the way that seafaring was viewed.

Henry II, between 1162 and 1167, decreed that the crew of his personal ship (a longship propelled by oars or sail) should wear a livery or uniform. He also made an allowance of 12d per day for the 'Naclerus', or Keeper of the Royal Ships, in Hampshire and Devon.

His son, Richard I, went further in developing the navy by creating the offices of 'Leaders' and 'Governer of all the King's Navy'. One hundred years later the offices of 'Admiral of the North' and 'Admiral of the South' were formed. Ninety years later, Edward, Earl of Rustano, was appointed Admiral of England, the office which would become 'Lord High Admiral'. Richard I became the first King since Alfred to lead a fleet into action when, during his third crusade, he invaded Cyprus.

During the thirteenth century, Edward I assembled what was, perhaps, the first 'national' fleet in Plymouth for a sortie against the French. In 1348 his grandson, Edward III, set sail with another fleet to maintain his grandfather's rights in Gascony. After the Battle of Poitiers he returned to Plymouth with the French king as his prisoner and half of France added to his kingdom. Some fifty years later, the French retaliated and thirty Breton ships, under the command of Le Sieur Du Chastel, sailed into the Cattewater and, following a fierce all-night battle, destroyed 600 houses in the area now known as Bretonside. Consequently, the Channel was patrolled by eight ships, between the dates of Candlemas and Martinmas, when prevailing winds from the south-west could carry unwelcome visitors to the English shores.

Edward III's ambitions to conquer France resulted in the Hundred Years' War. At the Battle of Sluys in 1340, 250 English ships, despite being outnumbered 3 to 1 by the French, managed to open an essential supply route for the invading English Army. The ships generally fought with bows and arrows, grappling and hand-to-hand fighting. Edward himself was wounded in the 'corg' *Thomas*. 1350 saw Edward III again at sea, this time with his son, 'The Black Prince', defeating the Spanish at the battle of 'Les Espagrols near Mer'. Edward III captured Calais in 1347 after a year's siege.

In 1415, 1,500 ships carried English forces across the Channel. Henry V built the first ship over 1,000 tons, the *Jesus*. A little later at Southampton, the 1,400-ton *Grace Dieu* was built. Some years later (in 1439) she was struck by lighting and destroyed by fire; her remains can still be seen in the river Hamble.

✐✐✐✐

When Henry VII came to the throne in 1485, the country was still reeling from the effects of the War of the Roses. Henry assisted the healing process by marrying Elizabeth of York, essentially combining the white and red roses of York and Lancaster. Despite this, his kingship remained shaky. By the end of his reign in 1509, however, he left a country at peace and with a full treasury. He started building the first dry dock in Portsmouth in 1495 and laid the foundations for the great changes that the Tudor monarchy was to witness. During the next 118 years there would be fundamental changes in the balance of power in Europe. There were two circumnavigations of the world and, in essence, the British Navy was born.

Henry's son and successor, Henry VIII, inherited a fleet of seven warships, and he built a further twenty-four including the ill-fated *Mary Rose*. He also created the Navy Board to oversee the fledgling Naval Service. Pay for the crews of naval vessels also dramatically increased during the Tudor period, from 18d per month for a seaman, rising to a princely sum of 10s per month in the reign of Queen Elizabeth I.

As mentioned, the first permanent royal dockyard was established at Portsmouth in 1496, during the reign of Henry VII. This consisted of a purpose-built dry dock that enabled warships to be hauled out of the water so that their hulls could be repaired and cleaned. Thereafter, further naval dockyards were built. Most of these were constructed along the banks of the rivers Thames and Medway, as here they would be ideally placed to defend the capital and to load ships with ammunition from the ordnance stores at the Tower of London. These yards were at Woolwich (constructed in 1512), Deptford (1513), Chatham (1570) and Sheerness (1665). In addition, two further, comparatively short-lived, yards were created at Erith (in existence from 1514 to 1521) and at Harwich (with a Navy Commissioner first appointed in June 1653). Of all the naval yards in this period, Chatham was undoubtedly the most important, with the vast majority of warships invariably given winter moorings in the Medway. This meant that any repair work was automatically undertaken at Chatham, with Sheerness merely supplying support facilities.

The difficult river approaches to these yards, combined with the increased size of the newer warships which had to navigate these hazards, eventually resulted in a decrease in the use of these yards. The Medway was particularly dangerous; several sandbanks and tortuous meandering approaches meant that ships often had to wait several weeks for the right wind conditions to be able to navigate it. Another reason for the decline of these south-eastern yards, and one which also had an impact on the fortunes of Devonport, is geography. Quite simply, during the sixteenth and seventeenth centuries, the enemy to English shores always appeared in the east, with the Dutch eventually emerging as the major rival to British maritime power. Things changed in the eighteenth century as the French became the most significant threat.

During the reign of Charles I, the possibility of siting a naval dockyard at Saltash had been explored. In 1625, Sir James Bagge had prepared the necessary plans but these were soon abandoned due to objections from the town's community, particularly the local fisherman who thought that the yard would affect their source of income. In the mid-seventeenth century there were establishments at Turnchapel and Teat's Hill for the 'breaming and repairing' of the king's ships. These were areas where the ships could be safely 'run aground', or at least hauled ashore so the necessary repairs could be carried out. As ships grew larger it became apparent that docks would have to be constructed to carry out this work. In 1677, Charles II ordered a report to be prepared, detailing the facilities available at Plymouth to support the fleet.

Any further plans for the building of a naval dockyard at Plymouth were put on hold as a result of the policies of James II and his attempts to turn the country towards Catholicism, which led to the Glorious Revolution of 1688 when James was deposed by his sister, Mary, and brother-in-law, William of Orange. When the Protestant William and Mary landed at Brixham in 1688, Plymouth was the first town in England to recognise William as king. At the end of November 1688, the ships which brought the new King and Queen to England sailed to Plymouth and wintered in the Cattewater. In the spring of 1689, King William rejoined his fleet and set sail for Ireland. Shortly after this an Act of Parliament was passed enabling the purchase of land that was deemed necessary 'for the defence of the dockyard, shipping in the harbour etc…' In June of that year, Plymouth was an advanced store base with its own storekeeper. Towards the end of the year the Admiralty was considering building a docking facility at Plymouth. The dock at Portsmouth was now some 150 years old, and the Channel had ceased to be the 'battleground' that it had been a few years previously.

Plymouth Sound and its various inlets and tributaries were surveyed in late 1689 by Edward Dummer, the Assistant Master Shipwright at Chatham. Dummer was not a stranger to the area, as he had been in charge of the facilities at Teat's Hill before moving to the east. His report suggested Point Froward as the ideal site for the dock, and this was soon approved by the government who subsequently instructed the Navy Board to build a single dry dock which would be capable of handling a third-rate ship. A Portsmouth mason, Robert Walters, tendered for this work in March 1690, and for a price of £11,000 he guaranteed that he would finish the dock within fifteen months. During this period, the possibility of siting the dock at Saltash was restated, this time in the slate quarry near the ferry but, as before, local opposition meant that the proposal was to be withdrawn. The contract for the Point Froward dock was signed on 3 December 1690. In a manner which was to typify the handling of government contracts to this day, no sooner had the contract been signed than Dummer changed the plans and proposed a more ambitious design. He suggested a bigger dry dock, that would be supported by a wet dock. He convinced the government that this new arrangement would have many advantages. However, the cost, which included stores, workshops and housing of the yard officers, had now escalated to £50,000. This revised plan was approved. The proposed site was owned by Mr Doidge and Sir Nicholas Morice. The young Sir Nicholas was the grandson of Sir William Morice MP for Plymouth and was a former Secretary of State and Privy Councillor to Charles II. Sir Nicholas's trustees (as he was just thirteen years old at this time) proved very difficult but eventually an agreement was reached, with the young Sir Nicholas receiving £139 and the Navy renting the land from him for £100 a year for seven years.

By 1692, the dock was completed and was used for the first time the following year. During 1692 William III inspected the site and pressed Parliament to increase the facilities available to the Navy. This resulted in a sum of £23,406 being voted to 'finish the yard'; this included the building of stores, workshops and accommodation for the dockyard officers. These officers were housed in an impressive row of houses, originally known as 'The Walk' but later became 'The Terrace'. The buildings were centred on the new dock and built 100ft above sea level. Another of the first buildings was a 60ft square storehouse known as 'the magazine'. The yard also had its own ropehouse; this impressive building was some 1,000ft long. Other buildings associated with rope-making were also built at this time, including the White Yarn House and the Tarred Yarn House.

The first ships built at the yard were launched in April 1694. These were two 73-ton 'advice' boats, *Postboy* and *Messenger*.

During the early years of the yard, the workmen lived on hulks in the river or in Plymouth itself; the owners of the land on which the yard was built, Sir Nicholas Morice and Mr Doidge, were unwilling to sell so the land continued to be leased. This problem was not resolved until 1700 when a few houses were built at North Corner – this was to become the town of Plymouth Dock. In 1718 the yard acquired 4½ acres of land to build a gun wharf – the area is now known as Morice Yard.

During 1727 the yard was significantly increased in size, when a further 20 acres of land was rented from Sir Nicholas. This new land was used largely as a mast pond and timber ground. New workshops were also constructed. In 1739 the yard had two dry docks and three building slips – these facilities turned out a large number of both new and rebuilt ships during the Anglo-Spanish war of 1739–1748. To enable the yard to carry out this work a recruiting drive was required to find the necessary shipwrights and caulkers. In the first of what was to become a pattern for both the navy and the yard, when the war ended in 1748 all the available berths in the Hamoaze were taken up by laid-up ships (in Ordinary). The Navy Board instructed the yard's workmen to stop working extra hours. On 5 July, twenty-nine riggers, forty-nine rigger labourers and twenty other workers were laid off. The next day a further eighty-one carpenters and 140 other workers left the yard. A year later, over 100 workmen were discharged after a visit by the Lords Commissioners of the Admiralty.

During 1758 a new dock was constructed to the north of the double dock. This dock was completed in 1763 and named Union Dock, after the first ship to enter it. In 1761, the dockyard area was increased to 70 acres by extending southwards by a further 10 acres. This area was known as New Ground and was used for building slips.

A slipway was built at the southern end of the yard in 1763, for the 'unloading of furze'. This was a brushwood used in breaming, the process whereby a ship's bottom is cleaned by burning off the marine growth. It was proposed to build a slip on this site and, in August 1774, plans were submitted for a building slip next to the boundary wall. The total cost for this was estimated to be £1,890 8s 2d. Southward extensions to the dockyard were complicated by the fact that the ropehouse was built at the original boundary of the yard in an east–west direction. The problem was dramatically resolved on the night of 2–3 July 1761 when a vast fire destroyed the building and most of its contents. Two new buildings were built on the site, the East and West Ropehouses. The East Ropehouse was used as a spinning house and the latter as a laying house. Other, smaller buildings were also constructed in the area, and these were also connected to the rope-making process: the White Yarn House, two Tarred Yarn Houses, Tarring and Wheel Houses. Also at this time, many of the original workshops and stores were demolished, and the Great Store House was replaced by a new building between the chamber and South Dock.

During the latter half of the eighteenth century, England was probably the wealthiest nation in Europe, due in no small part to overseas trade, particularly with the Far East.

Acts of Parliament in 1758 and 1766 authorised the building of fortifications to protect the dockyard and its surroundings. A wall and ditch were to be built around the yard and town. In the plans three gates were proposed to allow access to the yard, each of which was to have a drawbridge over the ditch. Work progressed slowly on the fortifications, which became known as the Lines. In 1816, the Duke of Wellington declared them unacceptable. Work was resumed in 1853, the ditch and wall forming the inner ring of Palmerson's folly, while the outer ring comprised a series of forts built at Bovisand and Picklecombe.

A powered magazine was built at Keyham Point in 1784. It was remote from other buildings in the yard – a prudent precaution, as the store could hold 20,000 barrels of gunpowder. One Friday afternoon during January 1821, this magazine blew up and two members of staff were killed.

In 1789 a new dry dock, the New North Dock, was completed. During the construction of the dock King George III visited. To honour the king's visit a small gazebo was built on King's Hill.

๑๑๑๑

The nineteenth century was a time of great change in Britain. Five years before Queen Victoria's coronation, the Great Reform Act saw the political parties strengthening their identities and the role of Prime Minister becoming more defined. Working conditions were improving, canals were being constructed, the railway network was growing, the Metropolitan Police Force was established and the Penny Post started. Once again, the Navy did not fare so well after the Napoleonic War; a force of ninety-eight ships of the line, manned by 130,000 officers and men was, cut to thirteen ships and 20,000 men two years later, in 1817.

During the 1820s the Navy took its first tentative steps with steam propulsion. In 1832 the Navy Board was merged into the Admiralty. In 1835 the first Chief Engineer and Inspector of Machinery was appointed. The first steam warship was built in the yard during 1831, the paddle steamer *Rhadamanthus*, designed by local Master Shipwright Thomas Roberts. As the number of steam-powered ships increased it became apparent that special facilities would be required and that the existing yard would need to be enlarged. A further 81 acres of land were acquired half a mile upstream from the original dockyard, and this area would house the new workshops and offices required to maintain the new steam fleet and increase the available wharfage and docks. Work commenced in September 1846 by George Baker & Sons on what would become known as Keyham Yard. In common with much government-funded work both past and present, cost over runs soon began to manifest themselves. Parliament was initially told that the project would cost £400,000, yet during September 1844 the contractor informed the

Admiralty that the work would cost £713,000 to complete. By 1848 this figure had grown to £1,225,000, and a year later the total cost stood at £1,322,627. A 6-acre area was developed to house the engineering department. This was known as the Quadrangle and was designed by Charles Berry, the architect who was also responsible for designing the Houses of Parliament. The workshops, housed under a glass roof, were built on three sides of open space and were built by prisoners who were housed in cells under the workshops. In addition to the production workshops, there were a number of supporting workshops; a leather shop, bottle test shop, lagging shop and a laundry.

In April 1855 work was started on constructing a tunnel to connect the two yards. This was completed in May 1857. Although prone to flooding, the tunnel did allow movement between the two yards possible without using the corporation land. By 1879 a narrow-gauge railway was installed in the tunnel.

In December 1859 Colonel Greene, accompanied by Mr Wilberforce, surveyed the land to the north of the existing yard with a view to extending the existing dockyard facilities. A plan was finally produced in 1890 – the proposed work would cost several million pounds but it was hoped that costs could be reduced by employing 'convict labour'. The proposal was delayed several times but work eventually commenced in February 1895. Approximately 3,500 men were employed during the building works, and a new residential area at Weston Mill had to be built to house them. The extension doubled the size of the existing dockyard, and of the 113 acres of development land only 35 were above the high water level – the rest had to be reclaimed from the Hamoaze. This involved constructing a cofferdam approximately 7600ft long, and removing over 4 million cubic yards of mud which was taken by barge and dumped a few miles beyond the breakwater. The extension provided two new basins, one tidal and one closed, and several docks. It was opened February 1907 at a final cost of £4,000,000. At the north-west corner of the extension a coaling facility was built. Although the work on the dock predominated in the early twentieth century, some other building work was also undertaken. In 1901, a new telephone exchange was built at Keyham, and a new surgery was also built along with new offices for the Chief Engineer. Central offices were built in 1911 and these provided accommodation for engineers, administration staff and the Captain of the dockyard, and were situated at the centre of the yard between Mutton Cove and the north end of the extension.

As the size of warships continued to increase during the early part of the twentieth century, various docks were developed to accommodate the larger ships.

During 1898, it was suggested that a canteen, run by the workmen, should be established in the yard. It was finally decided to build three canteens, one over the saw mill in the South Yard, one at Keyham and one at the new North Yard. The dining halls were run by the Devonport Dockyard Workmen's Canteen and Restaurant Association, and the first one was opened in 1913.

The assassination of the Archduke of Austria, Francis Ferdinand, on 28 June 1914, heralded the start of what would become the First World War. Eventually, on 4 August 1914, Britain declared war on Germany, a war which engulfed Europe over the following months and was to leave over 6 million men dead and 12½ million wounded. The dockyard was kept very busy during the war. In November 1914, the battle cruisers HMS *Inflexible* and HMS *Invincible* were made ready for an excursion into the South Atlantic to confront the German battle ships, under the command of Admiral Von Spee, which had sunk HMS *Good Hope* and HMS *Monmouth* two months previously. So urgent was the need to send the ships south that Winston Churchill, then First Lord of the Admiralty, decreed that, if necessary, 'dockyardmen' should be sent away with the ships, to return as opportunity may offer. The ensuing battle was Britain's only decisive naval victory of the war – only the German battleship *Dresden* escaped sinking.

A few days after the two battle cruisers left Devonport, HMS *Royal Oak* was launched. Originally designed as a coal burner, she was converted to oil during her construction, and she had the somewhat dubious honour of being the last battleship built at Devonport. Several submarines were also built during the war, including two of the infamous K-class – K6 and K7. Strangely, when K6 carried out her basin trail dive she refused to surface and was trapped on the bottom for two hours. Many 'Q' ships (merchant ships that had been fitted with concealed guns) were fitted out at Devonport. If one of these ships were attacked by a German submarine, some personnel would seemingly abandon ship. As the submarine closed in to finish off its victim, the gun crews would uncover their weapons and engage the enemy.

During the war the cold store depot was built, and it was initially used by the Ministry of Food. When the war ended it was no longer required and it became part of the Victualling Department.

The ending of the war in 1918 was greeted with mixed emotions in the yard. While there was gladness that the war was over it was tempered by concern for the future. During the war years, large amounts of money were paid in overtime payments. There were also fears that the dockyard staff would be reduced in the post-war conditions. Dr Macnamar, Parliamentary Secretary to the Admiralty, assured the Local Advisory Committee that it was in the Admiralty's interests to keep any changes to a minimum, and said that while there would probably be some redundancies (or 'discharges' as they were known) these would be small in number. He also stated that there was a lot of work 'overdue' from the war, including repair work and missed maintenance, to catch up with. The Admiralty was also looking at the possibility of the yard building merchant ships. However, just a matter of weeks later, 1,500 dockyard men received two weeks' notice. This was rescinded shortly after, as it was thought that the dockyard workers would join the railway men who were then on strike.

To try and resolve the problems facing the yard, several suggestions were put forward. These included bringing forward work on HM ships and short-time working. Despite opposition to reducing working hours in the yard, the government reduced the working week by several hours in January 1921. Full working hours (forty-seven hours a week) were resumed in September 1921. During 1919 a committee under the chairmanship of Lord Colwyn, which included the Mayor of Plymouth, was appointed by the Admiralty to consider the future use and management of the Royal Dockyards. They reported in December 1919, although the report was not made public for a further three months. In the committee's considered opinion, parts of the dockyard should not be leased to private companies, and although the dockyard could undertake the building of merchant shipping they thought that this was only a short-term solution to the yard's problems. The most controversial proposal was that part of the yard should be used as a terminal port, and a year later Mr Walter Long, First Lord of the Admiralty, stated that the Navy Board were willing to hand over the western arm of the Prince of Wales Basin for this use. There were several false starts to the dockyard's new career as a merchant ship-building firm, with several early orders not being accepted, but in the early 1920s the yard built two steamers for private owners. Several other ships were constructed, and a variety of other work was also undertaken at the yard. This included refitting trawlers that had been requisitioned during the war before they were returned to their owners, refitting the liner *Cap Polonia*, and work on completing several warships (among them submarine L54). All this undoubtedly eased the transition of the yard into a peacetime role.

There were several fires at the yard during the early 1920s. On 15 May 1920, a serious fire badly damaged No.1 store at Keyham. This building had been erected in the 1850s at No.3 basin. A year later, on 20 June 1921, there were three fires – the first in a submarine, and the second being a grass fire at Gun Wharf. Both of these were relatively minor and did little damage. The main problem with them was that they caused fire engines to be diverted from a far more serious fire in the South Yard, the hemp store. The building was all but gutted, but luckily the fire crews managed to stop the fire spreading to the ropery.

Due to the Navy's involvement in the War of Intervention in Russia, the run down of the fleet was delayed. Sir Eric Geddes, a former First Lord of the Admiralty, was appointed chairman of a committee in August 1921 that was to investigate national expenditure. Approximately a quarter of this report was dedicated to appraisal of the Navy Estimates. He and his committee concluded that the Royal Navy should be reduced by 35,000 officers and men, that this smaller navy would not need as many shore establishments, and that the estimates for expenditure in 1922–23 should be reduced from £81 million to £60 million. They also stated that 'The Royal Dockyards are so expensive that unless their costs can be brought more nearly to a commercial level, the work sent there should be reduced.' In fairness to the Admiralty, they did state that they thought comparisons were not appropriate and, with regard to repair work, which formed the bulk of the dockyards work, the comparisons were favourable. Sir Eric's recommendations became known as the 'Geddes Axe'; not the first and certainly not the last cleaver to be taken to the Navy and its support organisations as various governments attempt to balance the books.

Also taking place at this time, the Washington Treaty was signed, and this had effects which were as serious as, and longer-lasting than, the Geddes Axe. The US offered a ten-year 'break' in battleship construction by postponing the construction of fifteen capital ships, on condition that Britain and Japan took similar action comparable with the American proposal. Under the terms of the agreement Britain built two battleships, HMS *Nelson* and HMS *Rodney*, but neither of these ships was built at Devonport. During the 1920s and early 1930s, several cruisers were converted to aircraft carriers, and this work helped to reduce the number of workers laid off during this period.

∽∽∽∽

Even in the late 1930s, Britain and France still believed that Adolf Hitler could be placated and war in Europe could be avoided. Neville Chamberlain's trip to Germany in 1938 to meet the Führer did little more than buy another twelve months in which Britain could bolster its defences. The dockyard was considered a prospective target for air attacks, and so air raid precautions were put in place. On Sunday 3 September 1939, two days after the Germans invaded Poland, the British ultimatum expired and Britain and France were at war with Germany. On 29 September 1939, Winston Churchill, now appointed First Lord of the Admiralty, visited the dockyard. The yard was very busy preparing ships for war. In a strange parallel to the events of the First World War, a Devonport ship was dispatched to the South Atlantic at short notice to hunt German raiders. HMS *Exeter* left the dockyard in August 1939, and during December of that year she played a pivotal role in the Battle of the River Plate, along with HMS *Achilles* and HMS *Ajax*, during which the German pocket battleship *Admiral Graf Spee* scuttled herself rather than face, what she believed to be, superior British forces. HMS *Exeter* returned to Plymouth on 15 February 1940; Winston Churchill took the salute as the ship passed Mount Wise. The dockyard attracted the attention of the Luftwaffe, and Plymouth was first bombed during July 1940, with the heaviest raids occuring the following year, particularly during March and April. Damage throughout the yard was extensive, and amongst the worst-damaged buildings were:

The West Ropehouse, which was completely destroyed.
The East Ropehouse, which was very badly damaged.
Eleven houses in the Terrace which were destroyed.

The Mould Loft and church, which were destroyed.

The Scrieve Board, which was also damaged by incendiary devices but was saved by
 firewatchers.

No.1 store in the South Yard, which was destroyed. Unfortunately many of the yard's old
 records were stored there and these, along with a model of HMS *Hood*, were lost.

Despite the considerable damage throughout the yard, work was not seriously affected
and it is a tribute to the workforce, often working round the clock, that they managed
to complete several new builds and undertake a considerable amount of repair and
maintenance. During this period the yard built one aircraft carrier, one cruiser, six
submarines and carried out the repair of HMS *Exeter* and HMS *Ajax* after their
triumphant return from the River Plate.

The yard also undertook extensive reconstruction work on HMS *Belfast* after she was
damaged by a mine in the Firth of Forth in November, and prepared HMS *Campbeltown*
for the attack on St Nazaire. In the first eighteen months of the war alone, work was
carried out on over 200 destroyers.

∽∽∽

After the war, the Admiralty approached Plymouth Council with a proposal to acquire
182 acres of land at Devonport for future dockyard development. This was revised to 154
acres, and a year later it was announced that 78 acres would be sufficient for the yard's
future needs. The Admiralty later 'gave by' approximately 30 acres. The South Yard was
extended in a eastwardly direction to Chapel Street, while Keyham Yard was extended
to Devonport Park. During 1957 the dockyard church was rebuilt. Also during 1957, new
electrical workshops were built at Keyham on a site which had been blitzed. This was
named Goshen Yard, after one of the streets that had been destroyed in the Blitz.

A 'flyover' roadway was built in the mid-1960s, and this connected the three yards,
essentially making the one. This road link heralded the closing of the dockyard's rather
class-riddled internal railway. At various times it had up to six classes, ranging from
'Admiral' to 'Labourers', but whatever the class the passengers were, they made their
last journey on 16 May 1966. A little later this year the Albert Road Gate was closed. A
new wall was being built around the expanded yard so the gate was re-sited; the towers
remained and the clock was moved from its original tower to the one nearer the road.
During 1967 construction work started on the Apprentices' Training Centre in Goschen
Yard, and it was opened three years later, in January 1970. With the appointment of
Captain Southward as the General Manager for Devonport Dockyard in October 1966,
radical changes were made to the way the yard was managed, although Devonport was
the last of the Royal Dockyards to adopt this more functional management system.

The Defence Review of 1968 made a commitment to develop all four of the dockyards. This virtuous undertaking was complicated by a number of factors – the Dockyard Review, being undertaken at the same time, recommended that the yards be typed, i.e. ships of the same class would be 'base ported' in the same yard. It was proposed that the Leander-class frigates and their replacements would be based at Devonport. Devonport was also proposed as a base for the ever-growing nuclear submarine fleet, and would be a support base for their refitting and refuelling. The closing of many overseas bases made it necessary to review the support facilities for the UK fleet. To this end, a team was formed in 1969 which would evaluate and cost design options for: a frigate complex, nuclear facilities, and a fleet maintenance base. The plan proposed by this team was approved by the Admiralty Board in 1970, and Devonport Dockyard became known as Devonport Naval Base.

During December 1968, a committee was formed under the chairmanship of Sir John Mallabar. One of its aims was to examine the 'control and accountability of large scale MOD establishments'. The report was submitted some two years later, and in broad terms stated that the dockyards should not be privatised but should be managed on a commercial basis with, where possible, less input from the Navy. It also suggested that there should be competition with civilian yards and, if there was going to be a reduction in naval work, then it would be better to sell off one yard rather than try and run all four yards at reduced capacity. A month after the report was made public, Mr P. Kirk, Defence Under-Secretary for the Navy, had a meeting with MPs from the dockyard towns to reassure them that naval repair would not be contracted out and that all four Royal Dockyards were secure for the foreseeable future.

In January 1970, Dr David Owen, the Parliamentary Under Secretary of State for Defence (Navy), announced that a covered three-dock frigate refit complex would be built at Devonport as part of the dockyard modernisation plan. Numbers 5, 6 and 7 docks at Keyham were chosen for this project, which was completed March 1972.

During December 1970, work started in preparation for the arrival of the submarine squadron. Initially, North Lock was divided into two separate docks (11 and 12 docks), both capable of docking a nuclear fleet submarine. HMS *Valiant* was the first nuclear submarine to be docked, in December 1972. HMS *Otus* had docked earlier in the year as part of the proving trials. Work on the submarine refit complex began in 1975. This was a massive undertaking – either side of the main buildings is a dry dock, and at the landward end of the complex is the eight-storey management building. Behind this is the submarine support building, and four of its nine storeys are below ground level. The whole complex is dominated by the 80-ton crane. The complex was officially opened by HRH The Prince of Wales on 23 May 1980, and started its first refit, of HMS *Swiftsure*, in February of that year.

During this period much work was carried out to improve the facilities available in the yard. In June 1967, two new storehouses were built – one for paint and acids, the other for cables. A little later in the South Yard, a new office block was constructed; in March 1971 a new restaurant was opened; in April 1972 a new yard services workshop was completed in the North Yard, and a new medical centre was opened. In the first five years of the 1970s approximately £20 million was spent on new works.

During September 1979, the Secretary of State for Defence, Francis Pym, conducted several studies on defence spending. One of these studies was tasked with looking at the structure and organisation of the Royal Dockyards. The committee's report was published in a weighty two volumes and stated that the difficulties being experienced in the dockyards would be difficult to address. Apart from a decline in capacity it felt that the yard managers were still too tightly bound to the Navy and needed to be given more freedom to manage their yards. It also confirmed the need to keep all four yards. The various recommendations of the report were set to one side, however, when, in January 1981, the Secretary of State for Defence (who was now Mr John Knott) effectively decapitated the Royal Navy. In his Defence White Paper, he said that Britain's NATO contribution would be cut from fifty-nine ships to fifty, with some of these being held in reserve. It was announced a few weeks later that HMS *Invincible* would be sold to Australia, while all the Rothesay-class frigates, the County-class destroyers and several Leander-class frigates would be decommissioned. Meanwhile, HMS *Hermes* would be decommissioned three years early, in 1983, and the Antarctic survey ship HMS *Endurance* would be paid off, as would at least four RFA ships. He also announced that Chatham Dockyard would close and Portsmouth would be reduced to a minor repair yard. This would leave Devonport as the Royal Navy's only refit yard for both surface ships and submarines. Mr Knott was destined to make the same error of judgement of many of his predecessors. His colleagues barely had time to congratulate him on his rather innovative approach to defence management, when, out of the blue and totally unexpectedly, a group of Argentineans landed on a small island over 8,000 miles away and caused Mr Knott to radically reappraise his review and eventually forced him to resign.

The illegal landings were the precursor to the Falklands War. As it had so many times in the past, the yard did what was asked of it quietly and efficiently in a time of war. While the nation watched the country's armed forces set sail from Portsmouth, Devonport got on with its work. Conversion work on the ill-fated *Atlantic Conveyor* was completed in nine days. The *Atlantic Causeway* had a month's work completed in just eight days. The Sealink ferry *St Edmund* had two large helipads fitted within seven days, and, despite all the work in the yard, a number of men volunteered to join the task force as part of the Dockyard Repair Group. On 14 June 1982, the Argentineans surrendered and the fleet returned home to await the outcome of the inevitable peace dividend. Promises and lessons were soon forgotten and, despite reassurances that the country would retain a credible and strong armed service, politicians, ever conscious of saving a penny, soon began to whittle away at the services. In the aftermath of the Falklands War, with the removal of the financial restraints that were introduced prior to the 1981 Defence Review, a lot of development was carried out. Improvements were carried out in various factories, slips and basins were improved, new stores were built and accommodation was increased at the submarine refit complex to meet the requirements of the growing nuclear fleet.

On 6 April 1987, the dockyard was essentially privatised, and the company DML took over the management of the yard.

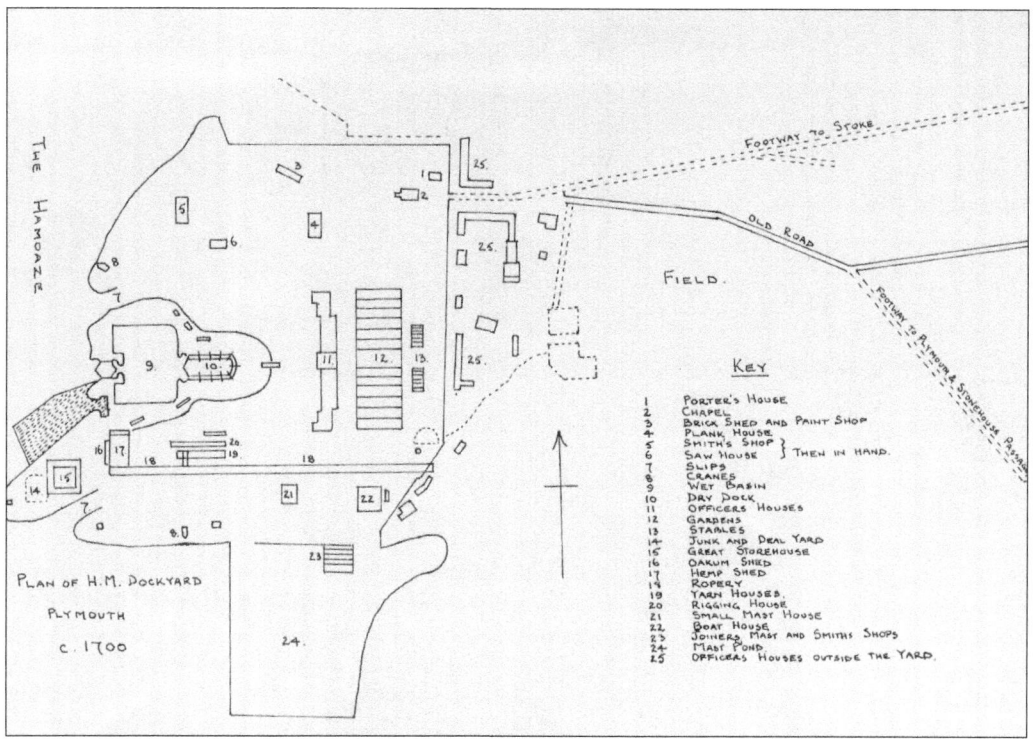

A plan of the original dockyard.

These houses, which overlooked the original dockyard, were occupied by the thirteen Yard Officers. These fine houses were badly damaged during the Second World War.

The summerhouse
on King's Hill.

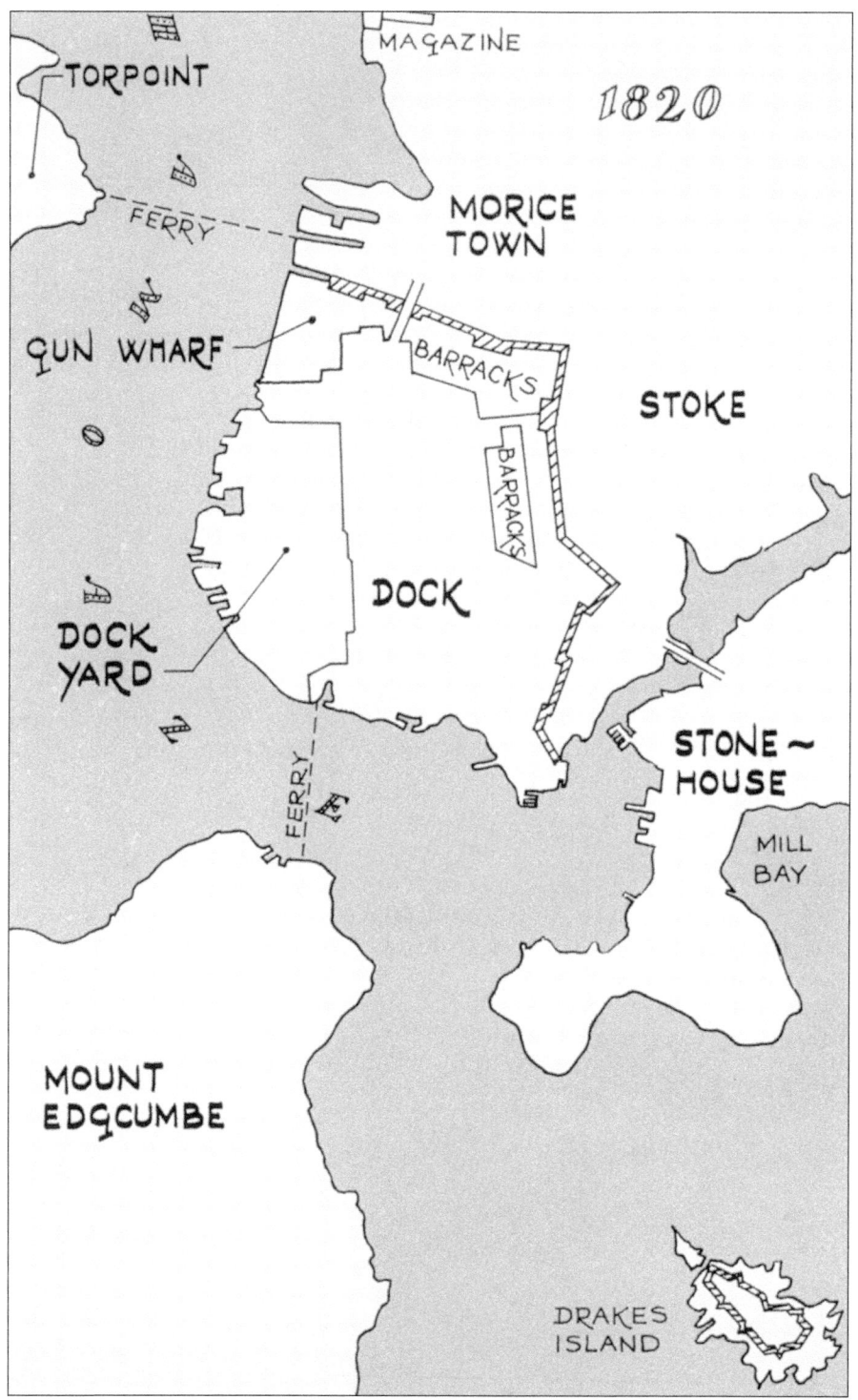

TORPOINT

MAGAZINE

1820

FERRY

MORICE
TOWN

GUN WHARF

BARRACKS

STOKE

BARRACKS

DOCK
YARD

DOCK

FERRY

STONE ~
HOUSE

MILL
BAY

MOUNT
EDGCUMBE

DRAKES
ISLAND

By 1820, the dockyard had been expanded by the addition of mast ponds and extra docks. At this time the workforce numbered about 2,000.

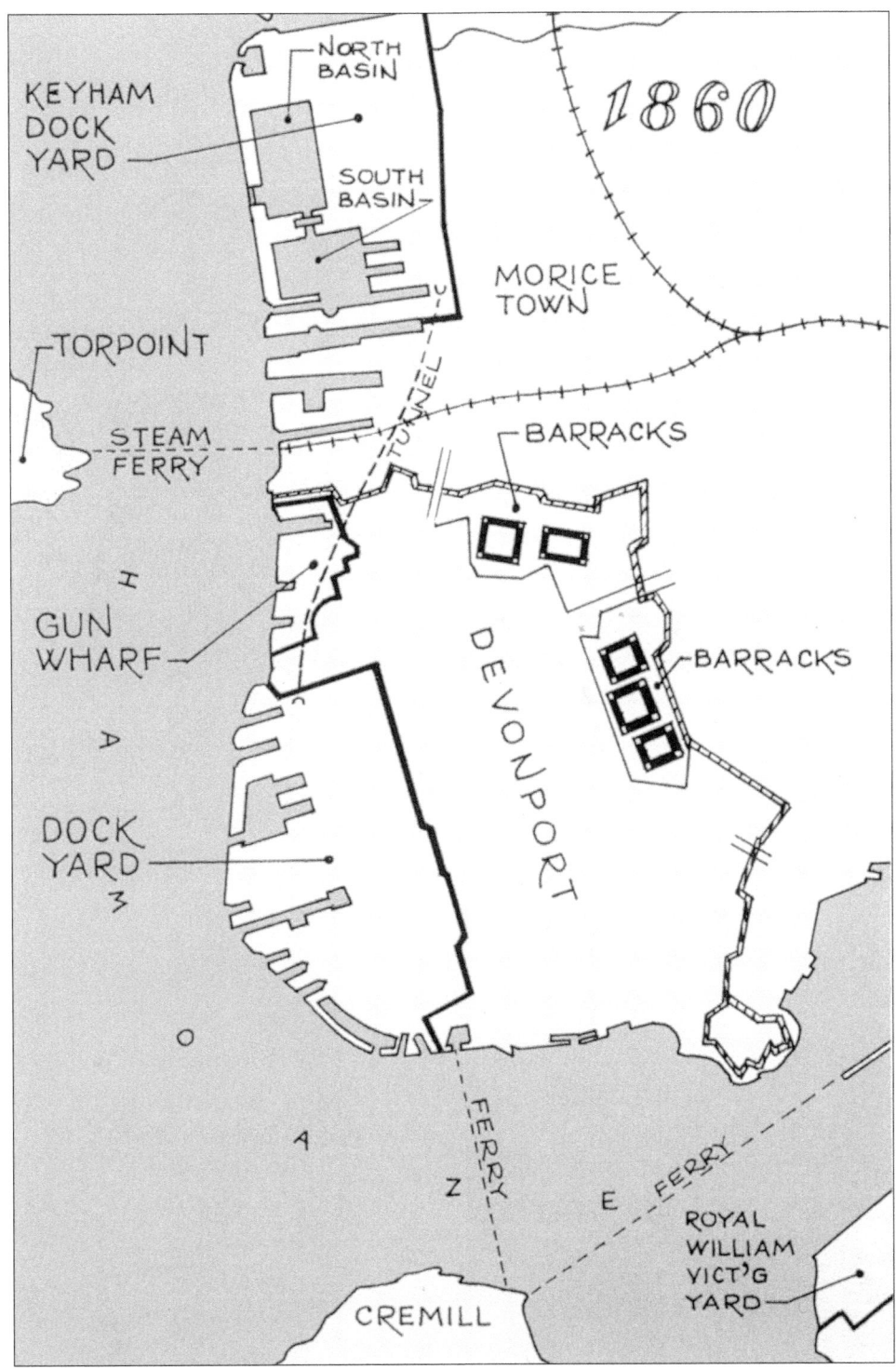

KEYHAM
DOCK
YARD

NORTH
BASIN

SOUTH
BASIN

1860

MORICE
TOWN

TORPOINT

STEAM
FERRY

TUNNEL

BARRACKS

GUN
WHARF

DEVONPORT

BARRACKS

DOCK
YARD

FERRY

E FERRY

ROYAL
WILLIAM
VICT'G
YARD

CREMILL

The opening of Keyham Dockyard by the Queen in 1853 further increased the size of the yard.

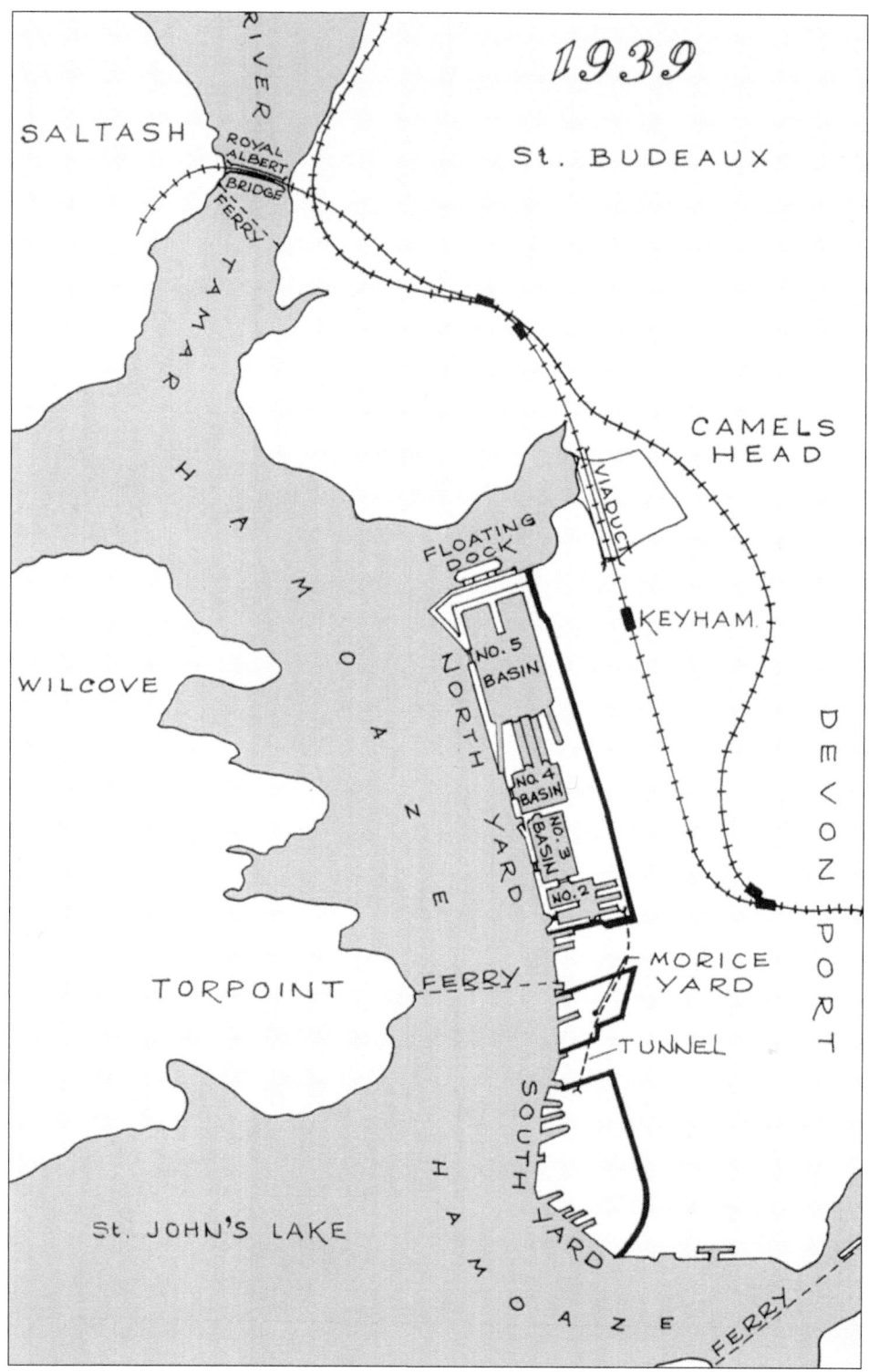

Plan showing North Yard and the newly constructed Nos 4 and 5 basins.

The old covered dock at Devonport.

HMS *Boxer* enters No.6 dock. The dock had to be extended to enable the newer classes of frigates to dock. The complex was completed in March 1972.

The South Yard in the 1990s.

The workshops.

The old covered slipways.

The headquarters building in 2002.

A Navy Day picture from the 1950s; the submarine is HMS *Rorqual*.

Looking north over the dockyard, the frigate complex can be seen in the right of the picture (1980s).

The frigate complex built at South Basin in the Keyham extension (1980s).

A general workshop scene from the 1940s.

The headquarters building at Devonport.

Ariel view of Weston Mill Creek, showing the submarine refit complex (1984).

Weston Mill Creek and the northern end of the dockyard before the submarine refit complex was built (1950s).

Launched on 5 July 1898, HMS *Ocean* was Devonport's first battleship. She had the somewhat unusual and unnerving experience of having 90ft of her bow collapse when a dockyard worker removed a bolt before anybody had finished the welding!

HMS *Superb* entering the submarine refit complex 19 April 1980.

Two

HMS DRAKE
THE ROYAL NAVAL BARRACKS, DEVONPORT

The time-honoured picture of the English sailor being kept a prisoner on his ship – poorly fed, beaten and rarely allowed ashore – does not really stand up to scrutiny. While life for the Victorian sailor was far from ideal, when compared to his shore-side compatriots it did have its advantages. He had at least one hot meal a day and, when he got it, his pay was generally better. There was no continuous service for men in the navy as we know it today. Men either volunteered or were press-ganged for a single voyage (however, one trip could often last for years). Lord Cochrane, in 1811, made a statement in the House of Commons in which he detailed the plight of HMS *Drake*, a 32-gun vessel with eighty-eight crew on board, who had been on continuous station in the Dutch East Indies for six years. As no pay was given until the end of the commission, the families the crew had left behind in England were probably suffering significant financial distress.

When ashore, the men were accommodated in hulks which were generally moored in rivers or estuaries close to the main naval ports. The hulk of *Defiance* was moored in the river Lynher while other hulks were moored off Torpoint, and some remained there well into the twentieth century. Life on board these hulks was austere at best, and by the 1850s their secondary purpose, to provide gunnery training, was no longer necessary. At this time the navy had several types of gun which it needed to train men to use, but the muzzle-loading guns on the hulks were hardly a suitable training aid.

It was decided, in the interest of providing better conditions for ratings, and hopefully to help retain the highly trained men, to build a purpose-built establishment ashore. Plymouth led the way, and construction of the naval barracks in Devonport, not far from the dockyard, in open countryside at the head of the Keyham Creek, commenced and was first occupied on 4 June 1889. It was originally named HMS *Vivid*, after the Commander-in-Chief's yacht, and an enthusiastic reviewer wrote:

> The Royal Naval Barracks at Devonport consist of a fine and substantially built group of stone buildings, and as viewed from the higher ground on the right of the road by which they are approached, present a pleasing picture.

Despite this pleasant picture, life in the new barracks still left a lot to be desired. For several years proper water supplies and other basic facilities were not available. Naval barracks were later built at Portsmouth, Chatham and other bases.

Britain was now experiencing a seemingly endless period of peace, punctuated only by minor skirmishes in various parts of the empire. Even these minor irritations could be viewed as an asset, as these rebellions were often dealt with by 'sending a gunboat', invariably commanded by a young officer – an excellent training opportunity.

David Beatty cut his teeth on such an expedition on the Nile, where he was said to have introduced a young Hussar named Winston Churchill to the heady delights of champagne.

The barracks hosted a grand ball, which was held in honour of the Commander-in-Chief, Admiral HRH Prince Alfred The Duke of Edinburgh (Queen Victoria's second son) in January 1891. At this sumptuous get-together, 1,200 guests are reported to have consumed a breathtaking 576 bottles of champagne, 540 bottles of spirits and 6,800 oysters! It is interesting and somewhat sobering to note that the catering bill was 7s 3d per head.

The clock tower of the barracks was completed in 1896, with four faces and a large bell for striking the hour. Originally it was driven by weights, which ran from the top of the tower to a considerable distance below ground level. These needed to be reset weekly, an arrangement that lasted until 1975. In its earliest days the tower also acted as a signalling tower. Semaphore arms were connected to the spire, enabling visual communication with the Naval HQ at Mount Wise.

To enhance the base's communication capabilities, in 1894 a loft was built in the barracks to house sixty homing pigeons. This well-intentioned but misguided stratagem failed as, despite intensive training, the pigeons kept getting lost.

The wardroom, which was 'probably the most magnificent building erected for naval purposes', was first occupied on 29 January 1903. In keeping with naval tradition, a grand ball was held to commemorate the opening. Captain H.S.F. Niblett and the twenty-eight officers hosted the ball, for which over 600 invitations were issued, although the amount of champagne and oysters consumed was not recorded.

The British Empire at this time was at the peak of its power and prestige. British ships carried 60 per cent of the world's trade, while 75 per cent of the world's shipping was built in British shipyards. The Empire and its trade routes were policed and protected by the Royal Navy, unbeaten in combat for several hundred years and supremely confident; probably its only real enemy was the British Government. In 1902, the newly crowned Edward VII visited Devonport for the ceremony of laying the keel of a new battleship bearing his name, whilst his consort, Queen Alexandra, broke a bottle of colonial wine on the bows of *Queen*, thereby launching that new battleship.

Afterwards, the king and queen visited the naval barracks, being driven to the parade ground in a carriage and four, for a ceremony attended by 9,650 officers and men. The king presented 280 China and sixty South African medals following the recent end to the Boxer Rebellion and the Boer War.

In 1928 the first 'Navy Days' were held, and a few years later another event happened that was to continue to the present day. On 31 July 1933, a dinner was held to celebrate Drake's victory over the Spanish Armada. The dinner continues to be held annually and it is said that it was at this inaugural dinner that it was decided to rename the barracks HMS *Drake*. On 1 January 1934, the new name became official.

During the Second World War the barracks were badly damaged when, on 21 April 1941, Boscawen Block was bombed. Over 100 people were killed.

∽∽∽

In April 2008 the Princess Royal opened a multi-million pound new accomodation complex at HMS *Drake*, which will provide single-living facilities for all.

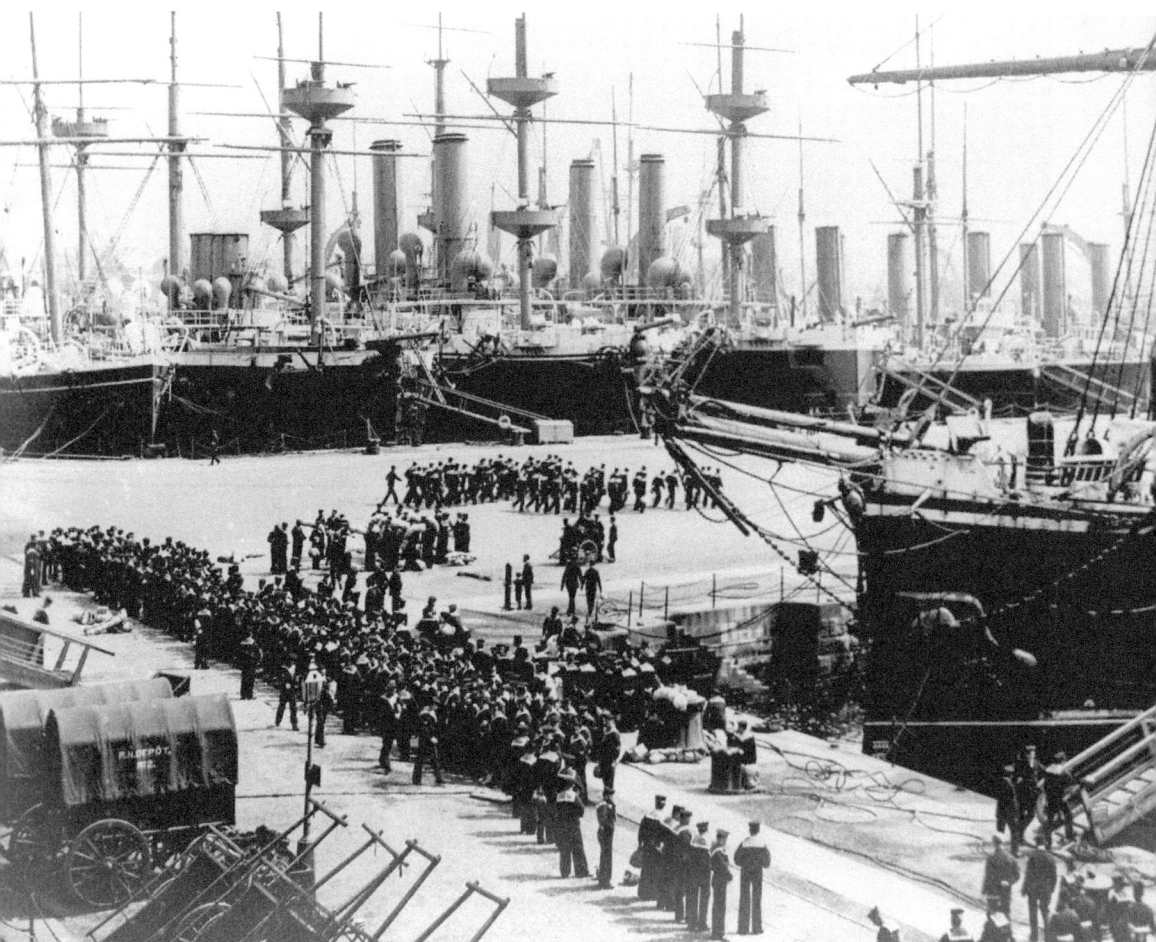

Mustering ships' companies in the dockyard (1890).

Kit muster (early 1900s).

Torpedo instruction (early 1900s).

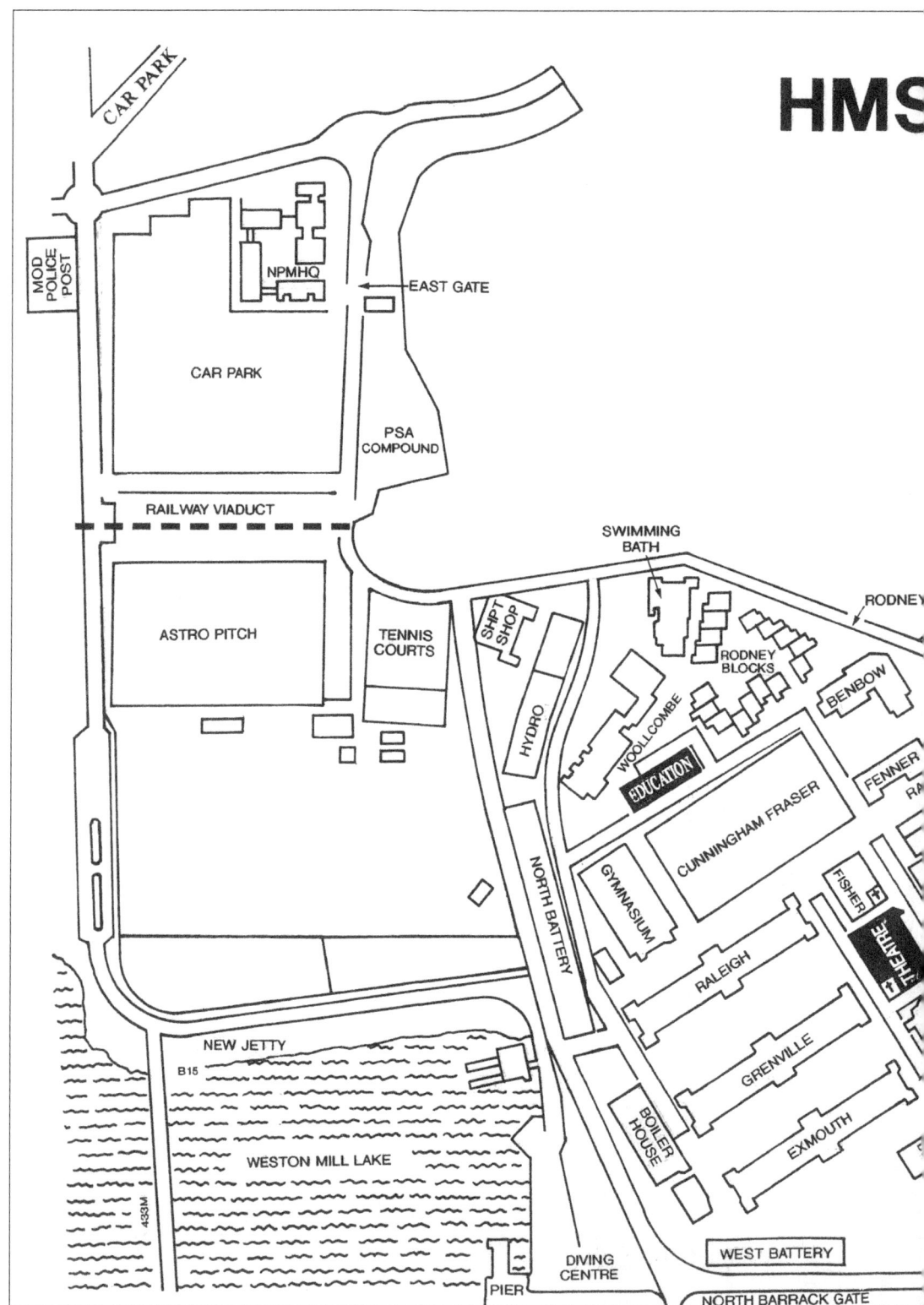

HMS

CAR PARK

MOD POLICE POST

NPMHQ

EAST GATE

CAR PARK

PSA COMPOUND

RAILWAY VIADUCT

SWIMMING BATH

RODNEY

ASTRO PITCH

TENNIS COURTS

SHPT SHOP

HYDRO

RODNEY BLOCKS

BENBOW

WOOLLCOMBE

EDUCATION

CUNNINGHAM FRASER

FENNER

RA

GYMNASIUM

FISHER

THEATRE

RALEIGH

NORTH BATTERY

GRENVILLE

NEW JETTY

B15

BOILER HOUSE

EXMOUTH

433M

WESTON MILL LAKE

PIER

DIVING CENTRE

WEST BATTERY

NORTH BARRACK GATE

DRAKE

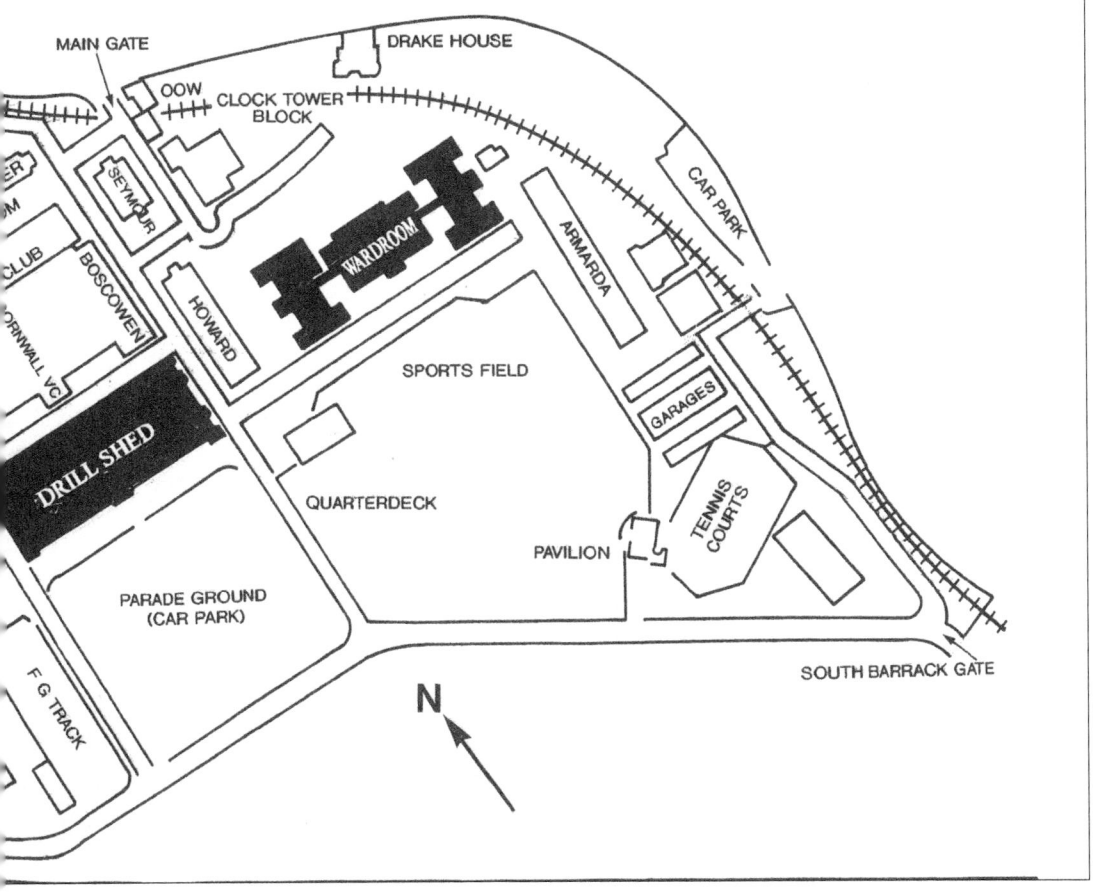

MAIN GATE

DRAKE HOUSE

OOW CLOCK TOWER BLOCK

SEYMOUR

BOSCOWEN

HOWARD

CLUB

CORNWALL VC

WARDROOM

ARMARDA

CAR PARK

GARAGES

DRILL SHED

SPORTS FIELD

QUARTERDECK

PAVILION

TENNIS COURTS

PARADE GROUND (CAR PARK)

F G TRACK

N

SOUTH BARRACK GATE

Drake montage.

Officers of HMS *Exmouth* (1880s).

Torpedo tubes (admittedly, on a surface ship). Trainable torpedo tubes were fitted to surface ships, presumably because our General Service counterparts could not do the clever sums like us submariners!

The barracks at HMS *Drake* (c.1930).

On this page and those that follow are various aerial views of HMS *Drake*, dating from the 1950s and 1960s.

Three

HMS
DEFIANCE

SECOND TO NONE

The first *Defiance* was launched in 1588 and saw action against the Spanish Armada. She was a pinnace of between 40 and 80 tons, lateen-rigged and could be propelled by oars. The second *Defiance* (1590–1650) was a 500-ton 'improved galleon' design. She was with Drake in the West Indies, and Drake was buried from *Defiance* in Nomore de Dois Bay on 29 January 1591, thus beginning the association between *Defiance* and Plymouth.

In all, there have been thirteen ships named *Defiance*. The tenth one, a third-rate ship of 74 guns, fought at Trafalgar. The twelfth ship was a second-rate screw vessel of 5,270 tons. She was launched at Pembroke in 1861, but her main armament was not fitted, and she was towed to Plymouth and laid up. In 1884 she was commissioned as the Devonport Torpedo School under the command of Cdr J. Norcock. She was moored off Wearde Quay at Saltash and was later joined by HMS *Inconstant*, which acted as an accommodation ship. In the finest traditions, a parade round was built ashore, and a short time later the GWR built a station, Defiance Halt. This establishment was disbanded in 1930 and re-established later in the same year at Wilcove. HMS *Inconstant* was the only remaining ship from the original group, and she was joined by the cruiser HMS *Andromedia* and the submarine depot ship HMS *Vulcan*. The lecture rooms and officers' accommodation were in HMS *Andromedia*, while the cramped and airless mess decks, where the trainees slept in hammocks, were spread over three ships. Up to the war, electricity for the establishment was supplied by HMS *Vulcan*'s primitive generators. Eventually, the ships were connected to shore supply, but at best the power was variable, and the lighting ranged from a barely glowing bulb to almost searchlight intensity.

Perhaps it was because they had to absorb the mysteries of underwater warfare and the complexities of electricity and electronics in these somewhat primitive conditions that *Defiance* men considered themselves superior to all others. They used to say that a *Defiance* Seaman Torpedoman (the lowest grade) equalled a Pompey Torpedo Instructor (the top of the tree). The school continued until 1947, when it became known as the TAS and Electrical School. It was finally closed in 1959, and the school was moved into the barracks during 1956.

Apart from producing the finest Torpedomen in the fleet, HMS *Defiance* had another claim to fame. It is said that *Defiance* was the home of naval radio. Cdr Jackson was experimenting at the same time as Marconi, using similar equipment – the spark transmitter and coherer receiver – and some said that he reached the goal first, although Marconi was the first to the Patent Office. It seems that the Commander hoped to form a screen of radio – guiding torpedoes that would precede the fleet. In 1907 he made an experimental broadcast from Mount Wise to HMS *Defiance*, and when listeners were asked what they heard, they said it sounded like someone playing the piano. It would appear that the Commander preceded Jimmy Young by several decades.

On 17 February 1960, HMS *Forth*, a submarine deport ship that had undergone a four-year refit to enable her to support nuclear submarines, was re-commissioned as HMS *Defiance*. She was to be the depot ship of the 2nd Submarine Squadron that had been based in Devonport since February 1969, having moved there from Portland.

It was intended that the facilities provided by the ship – workshops offices etc. – would eventually be provided ashore. These were finally completed early in 1978, and the Fleet Maintenance Base, or HMS *Defiance*, was commissioned on 21 April 1978 by the then Prime Minister, The Right Honourable James Callaghan MP. The establishment compared favourably with a well-equipped civilian engineering works. It had modern machine shops, carpenters, cutting and welding bays and so on. In addition, it has specialised workshops for repairing equipment such as periscopes, electronic equipment and computers, and, because it was intended to base a nuclear submarine squadron here, it had special facilities for carrying out nuclear repairs in submarines. All these departments were supported by a stores and administrative organisation and by quality assurance and health and safety departments.

Within the base the men were divided into groups specialising in different classes of ship and submarines.

The base was commanded by the Captain Fleet Maintenance (Captain J. Burgess MVO Royal Navy). In addition to being the Commanding Officer, Captain Burgess was tasked with providing engineering and staff support to operational ships and submarines, and representing the Commander-in-Chief's interests in those ships being refitted. To help him achieve this he had a staff of approximately 1,000 men and women. The majority of these were from the technical branches of the Royal Navy although there were also a small number of specialists drawn from the executive, medical and supply branches.

HMS *Defiance* was finally 'absorbed' into HMS *Drake* in July 1995.

Submarines of the 2nd Submarine Squadron alongside HMS Defiance (1992).

Workshops of HMS *Defiance*. Nice to see the submariner made the effort for the photograph!

HMS *Defiance* with submarines alongside.

SECOND TO NONE

HMS *Defiance*'s crest.

Looking through the periscope (1932).

Moored off Wearde Quay, the torpedo school HMS *Defiance* is to the right while the ship on the left is *Inconstant*, which was used as an accommodation ship from 1920. The establishment was disbanded at Wearde Quay and reformed at Wilcove in 1930.

Sailors on 'Defiance Platform', which served as an arrival point for men joining HMS *Defiance*.

The path leading from HMS *Defiance* up to the railway station; a route well worn by sailors.

Loading a torpedo (2001).

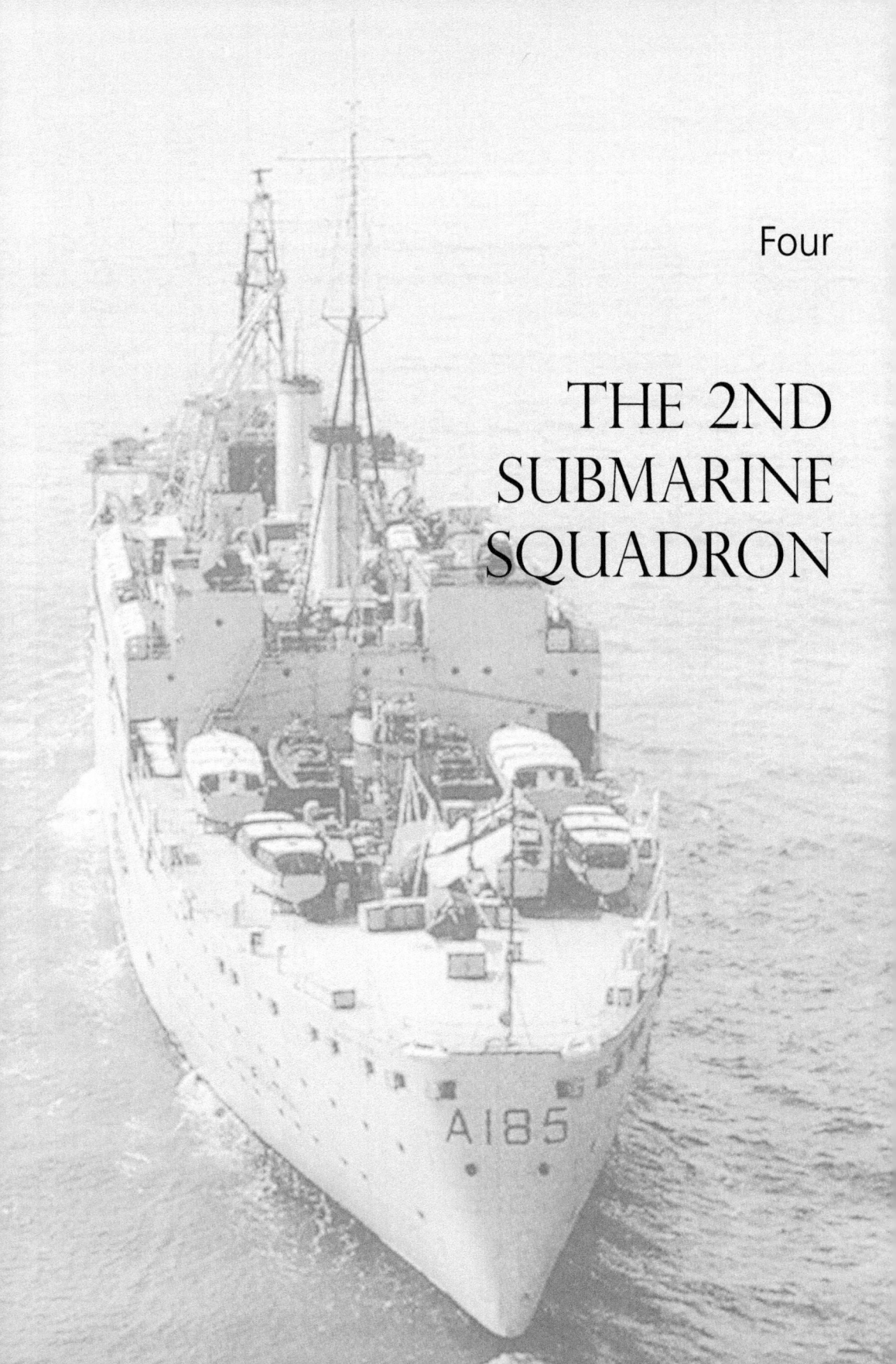

Four

THE 2ND
SUBMARINE
SQUADRON

By 1900, the American, French, Russian and Turkish navies considered the submarine to be a viable weapon and were building up flotillas of these new vessels. In the summer of 1900, Isaac Rice from the American Boat Company arrived in the UK, essentially on a sales visit. His company owned the patents for the Holland submarine design and he was hoping to interest European countries in the designs. Lord Rothschild introduced Rice to members of the Admiralty and, as a result, before the end of the year it had been agreed that Vickers & Son and Maxim Ltd at Barrow-in-Furness would build five submarines, utilising the Holland design, for the Royal Navy. This was a rather radical change of naval policy. The Controller, Sir Arthur Wilson, was of the opinion that submariners should be hung as pirates, and the change of policy direction was explained by the fact that the submarines were being acquired to train destroyer captains in anti-submarine tactics.

The first submarine flotilla to be formed at Devonport was the 10th Flotilla in November 1910. By 1914, it had been renamed the 1st Flotilla and was based on the depot ship HMS *Onyx*. Two of the flotilla submarines were lost; A9 under the command of Lt G.S. Walsh, when it collided with SS *Coath* off Plymouth and foundered, and A8, which was running on the surface in the Sound when water flooded in. In the resulting battery explosion fifteen men died, while four managed to escape.

The 2nd Submarine Flotilla was originally formed at Portsmouth, and was based on the depot ship HMS *Bonaventure*. It comprised of E10, D2, S1, A5, A6, A13, and B1. By 1916 the flotilla, which by now consisted of eight C-class submarines, was on the Tyne, still based on HMS *Bonaventure* and under the command of Cdr MK de M. Burgess. At the outbreak of the Second World War the flotilla was in Dundee, but as a result of the fear of air attacks it was moved to Rosyth with HMS *Forth* in April 1940, under the command of Capt. G.C.P. Menzies. It was briefly reformed at Malta during the Second World War. Thereafter, it was based at Portland until moved to Devonport.

Depot Ships of the 2nd Submarine Squadron

April 1909–August 1912	*Bonaventure*
August 1912–August 1916	*Dolphin*
August 1916–September 1918	*Bonaventure*
March 1919–December 1919	*Ithuriel*
December 1919–May 1939	*Lucia*
May 1939–September 1941	*Forth*
August 1944–December 1945	*Wolfe*
September 1947–April 1958	*Maidstone*
April 1958–July 1960	*Tyne*
November 1960–October 1962	*Forth*
October 1962–April 1970	*Adamant*
April 1970–February 1972	*Tyne*
February 1972–July 1995	*Defiance*
July 1995–Present	*Drake*

Submarine A8 sank in Plymouth Sound while running on the surface, when water flooded through an open hatch and the battery exploded. Fifteen of the crew were lost, four escaped (1914).

Opposite: HMS *Maidstone*, depot ship of the 2nd Submarine Squadron from 1947 to 1958. She was later converted in Portsmouth Dockyard to enable her to act as a depot ship for nuclear submarines.

ERA's coalship party (1880s).

Opposite: Submarines of the 2nd Submarine Squadron alongside their depot ship.

Holland 1. She was scrapped in 1913 but sank off Eddystone. She was located by HMS *Bossington* during 1981.

A submarine entering No.5 basin (1997).

HMS *Astute* enters Aden on her way home to Plymouth during 1965.

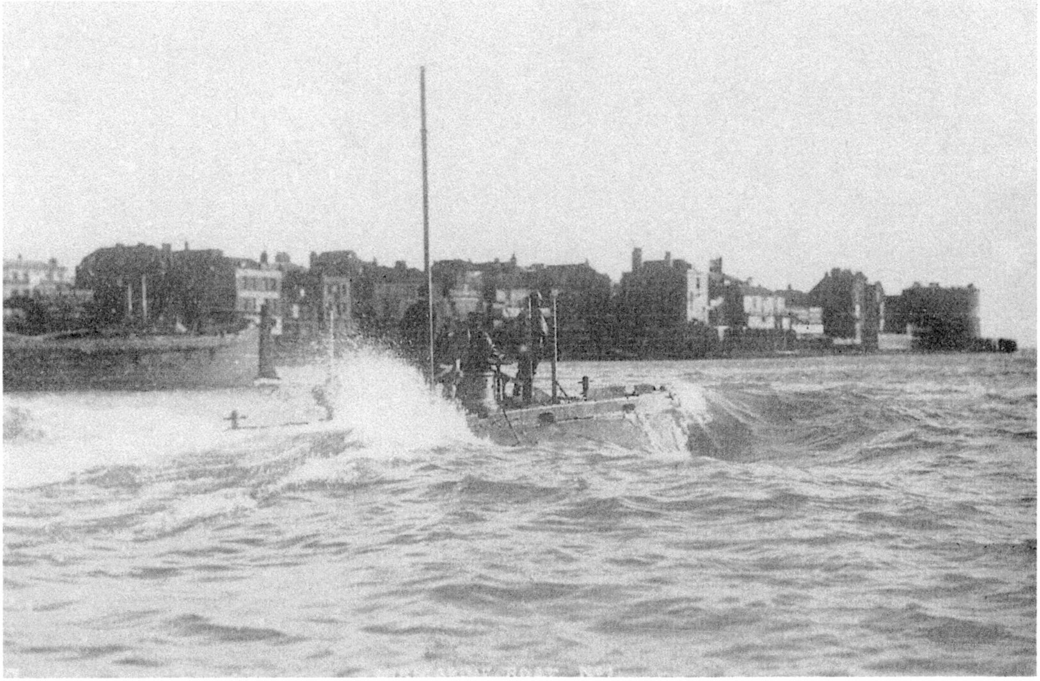

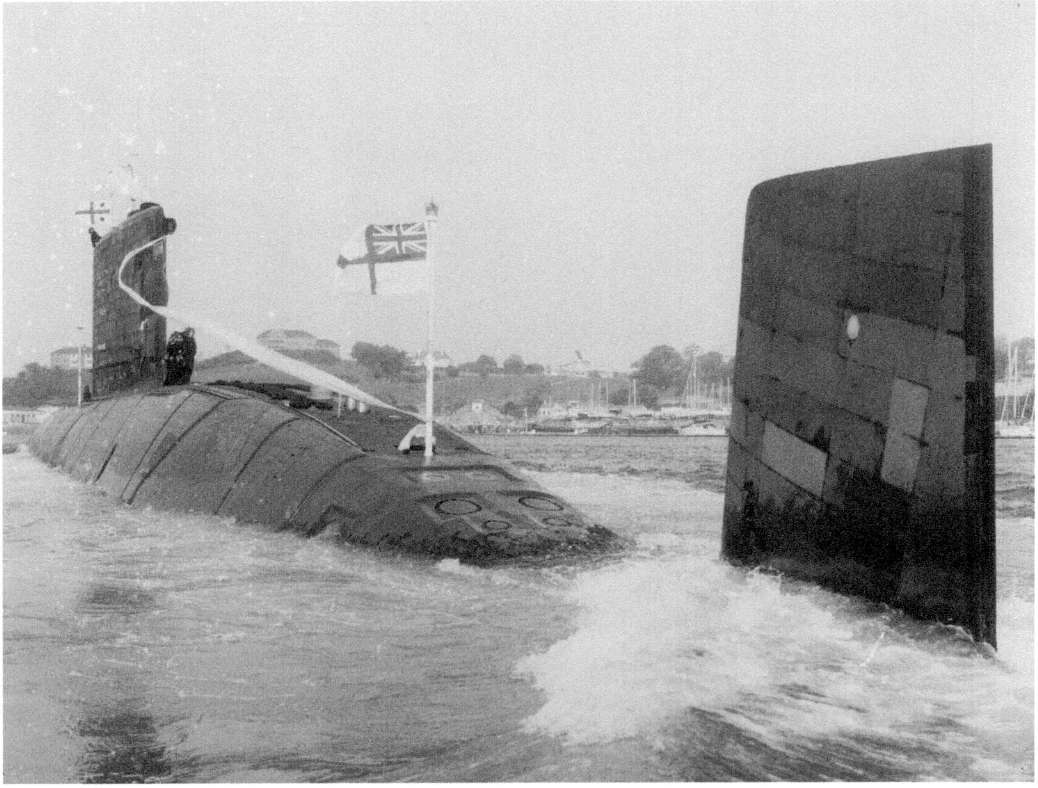

HMS *Lucia*, the depot ship of the 2nd Submarine Squadron between 1818 and 1939.

Opposite above: Submarine Boat No.2 off Devonport during 1904.

Opposite below: A submarine from the 2nd Submarine Squadron paying off.

Submarine support ship HMS *Diligence*.

Opposite above: In October 1976, HMS *Sovereign* surfaced at the North Pole.

Opposite below: HMS *Sea Scout* at Navy Day, 1961.

HMS *Triumph* in the dockyard.

Opposite above: Submarine alongside the refit complex.

Opposite below: HMS *Trenchent* and USS *Spadefish* at the North Pole in 1992. Note the RAF trying to muscle in on the picture!

HMS *Vanguard* entering the V-boat refit complex (1995).

A submarine undergoing refit in the submarine refit complex.

Opposite above: HMS *Triumph* arrives at HMAS Stirling in sunny Australia in 1993. When she returned to Devonport she had been away for 197 days; 151 of these had been spent at sea, of which 131 were spent underwater.

Opposite below: HMS *Torbay* at No.10 dock.

HMS *Odin* alongside.

Opposite above: HMS *Sceptre* moving out of the dock in November 1986.

Opposite below: HMS *Oppertune* undocking.

A T-class submarine being manoeuvred in the river.

Opposite above: HMS *Olympus* undergoing a stability test during May 1984.

Opposite below: HMS *Achetes*, built at Devonport and launched by Lady Leatham, wife of Admiral Leatham. (CC Plymouth)

HMS *Defiance* and the submarine refit complex.

Above and below: Decommissioned nuclear submarines laying alongside prior to final disposal.

BIBLIOGRAPHY

Allaway, Jim, *More Navy in the News 1954–1994*, (HMSO: London).

Burns, Lt Cdr K.V., *The Devonport Dockyard Story*, (Maritime Books: Cornwall, 1984).

Endacott, Andy, *Naval Heritage in the West Part I*, (D.L. Endacott: Cornwall, 1986).

Endacott, Andy, *Naval Heritage in the West Part II*, (D.L. Endacott: Cornwall, 1987).

Endacott, Andy, *300 Years 'Devotion to Duty'*, (D.L. Endacott: Cornwall: 1991).

Other titles by the same author

Clyde Submarine Base
 ISBN 978 0 7524 1657 1

HMS Dolphin: *Gosport's Submarine Base*
ISBN 978 0 7524 2113 1

Submariners: Real Life Stories From the Deep
ISBN 978 0 7524 2809 3

Other titles published by The History Press

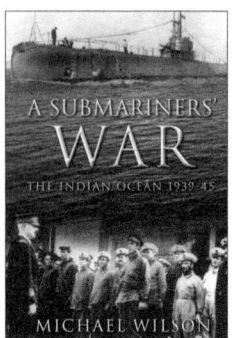

A Submariners' War: The Indian Ocean 1939–1945
MICHAEL WILSON

Michael Wilson, an ex-submarine officer, presents an authoritative account of Second World War operations in the Indian Ocean – an area of the world where, uniquely, the submarines of Great Britain, the Netherlands, the USA, France, Italy, Germany and Japan all operated and fought during the war. He uses archive material from all the countries involved and looks at the overall picture of how the submarines were deployed and the level of success they achieved.

978-1-8622-7458-7

The Industrial Archaeology of Docks and Harbours
MICHAEL STAMMERS

The United Kingdom, as a set of offshore islands, has always depended on the sea for transport. 95 per cent of all our trade by volume, whether imports or exports, is carried across the sea by ships. Today, such sea trade is mainly concentrated in large or specialised ports and the smaller ports have tended to decline hosting no more than inshore fishing and pleasure craft. This book is a history of port development in the United Kingdom, with examples of the main structures drawn from ports all around the coast.

978-0-7524-3900-6

Submariners: Real Life Stories from the Deep
KEITH HALL

The Senior Service has, for 100 years, had submarines. Originally thought to be 'un-English', submarines helped the British to win two world wars and have played a great part in Britain's nuclear deterrence programme. Their crews are a breed apart. The danger of their missions drew submariners together and helped create the spirit of camaraderie that is revealed in this book.

978-0-7524-2809-8

Falmouth Haven: The Maritime History of a Great West Country Port
D.G. WILSON

This work attempts to bring the old shipyards and tide mills of the area back to life, and place the Bar in its rightful place within the broader history of a great West Country port. David Wilson has had many years of experience in amateur archaeology, local history studies and sailing traditional craft. Illustrated with over 150 photographs, *Falmouth Haven* will appeal to lovers of maritime history and those with an interest in the Falmouth area.

978-0-7524-4226-6

If you are interested in purchasing other books published by The History Press, or in case you have difficulty finding any History Press books in your local bookshop, you can also place orders directly through our website

www.thehistorypress.co.uk